JUV
KF
8742
.Z9
K76
1996

Kronenwetter,
Michael.

The Supreme Court of
the United States.

American Government in Action

The Supreme Court of the United States

Michael Kronenwetter

ENSLOW PUBLISHERS, INC.
44 Fadem Road   P.O. Box 38
Box 699   Aldershot
Springfield, N.J. 07081   Hants GU12 6BP
U.S.A.   U.K.

Library of Congress Cataloging-in-Publication Data.

Kronenwetter, Michael.
    The Supreme Court of the United States / Michael Kronenwetter.
       p. cm. — (American government in action)
    Includes bibliographical references and index.
    Summary: Discusses the history, powers, and duties of the
nation's highest judicial body and includes a chapter on politics
and the Court and another on historic decisions.
    ISBN 0-89490-536-8
    1. United States. Supreme Court—Juvenile literature.
[1. United States. Supreme Court.] I. Title. II. Series.
KF8742.Z9K76 1995
347.73'26—dc20   95-13477
[347.30735]   CIP
                            AC

Printed in the U.S.A.

10 9 8 7 6 5 4 3 2 1

Illustration Credits:
Collection of the Supreme Court of the United States, pp. 29,
32, 36, 38, 40, 48; Franz Jantzen, Collection of the Supreme
Court of the United States, pp. 4, 61, 62; Harris & Ewing,
Collection of the Supreme Court of the United States, pp. 13,
42; Library of Congress, pp. 8, 26, 82; National Geographic,
Collection of the Supreme Court of the United States, pp. 50,
52.

Cover Illustration:
Collection of the Supreme Court of the United States

Contents

The inscription chiseled above the front entrance of the Supreme Court building reads "equal justice under law."

Preface

Washington, D.C., is a city of magnificent public buildings—imposing symbols of the hope and power represented by the United States of America. Tourists from all over the world flock to view the great memorials of America's past: from the optimistic splendor of the Washington Monument to the grim remembrance of the Vietnam Veterans Memorial. But the real glory of the national capital is in its living landmarks—the centers of activity and power, inside which the U.S. government conducts its business.

The most popular tourist attractions are the White House and the U.S. Capitol, where the President and Congress do their work. These buildings inspire awe in almost everyone who enters them, because of the immense importance of what goes on there. But no building in Washington is more truly impressive to people who understand how the U.S. government actually works than the white marble home of the Supreme Court of the United States.

"The Republic endures," declared Chief Justice Charles Evans Hughes, as he helped lay the cornerstone of the building in 1932, "and this is the symbol of its faith."[1] More than any other building in Washington, the Supreme Court represents the effort that makes the United States the hope and envy of people around the world. That aspiration is chiseled in marble above the broad steps leading to the front entrance of the Court—EQUAL JUSTICE UNDER LAW.

Guarding
the Ideal

The nine Justices who sit on the United States Supreme Court are the guardians of that great ideal of equal justice under law. Their job is to see that the rights of all Americans are protected—young and old, rich and poor, the powerful and the powerless—no matter what their color, creed, or background. This is an enormous responsibility, and one that can probably never be fulfilled completely. But it is the ideal of the American judicial system—and, most particularly, the job of the U.S. Supreme Court—to try.

The Justices have enormous power to go with their enormous responsibility. In a sense, the Court is the most powerful of the three branches of the government, because it can stop the other branches

The Justices of the Supreme Court have enormous responsibility, including the duty to uphold the United States Constitution.

from abusing the people's rights. The Court can overturn any law passed by a state, or by the Congress itself, which it believes violates the U.S. Constitution. Under some circumstances, it can tell state governments, the Congress, and even the President of the United States what to do.

At times, it can do even more. It can transform American society itself. That is what it did on May 17, 1954—the day it announced its decision in the case known as *Brown* v. *Board of Education*.[1] It was the *Brown* decision that declared segregation—the legal separation of the races—to be unconstitutional in the schools of the United States.

▶ Jim Crow

Until *Brown*, an unclimbable wall of segregation kept whites and blacks apart in much of the United States, particularly in the South. It was not just that social contact between African Americans and other citizens was discouraged. Separation of the races, as it was called, was enforced by a whole system of state and local laws that forbid blacks to use the same public facilities as whites.

Among other things, these so-called "Jim Crow laws" decreed that blacks and whites could not marry each other. They could not live in the same neighborhoods, or even stay in the same hotels. They could not eat in the same restaurants, drink from the same water fountains, or use the same restrooms. And they could not attend the same schools.

Jim Crow was a way of keeping blacks down, and assuring that whites would stay in a privileged position. For a short time after the slaves had been freed in the Civil War, the North had imposed a period of Reconstruction on the South. Federal troops protected the rights of blacks, as they competed with whites in ways they had never been able to as slaves. They not only started businesses, but took over many government offices that the federal government closed to whites who refused to give allegiance to the Union.

The experience of Reconstruction angered and frightened many southern whites. They had always thought of themselves as naturally superior to the African Americans they had kept in bondage for generations. Financially well-off whites had simply assumed that the wealth and power of the region would belong to them forever. Even the poorest whites had been able to look down on black people, and to know that, no matter how miserable they were themselves, at least they were better off than the slaves. Now, however, whites of all social classes were faced with the possibility that they might have to share not only their wealth and power, but even their social status, with the ex-slaves.

Once Reconstruction was over, the Union troops returned home and left the South to its own devices. The white southerners quickly retook power, and in the process, they enacted Jim Crow laws to keep blacks "in their place."

White southerners insisted that segregation did not hurt anyone. It was purely a matter of preference, they said. Whites preferred to be with whites, and blacks preferred to be with blacks. What was wrong with some public facilities being reserved for whites, as long as blacks had public facilities of their own? But African Americans pointed out that the facilities reserved for them were invariably inferior to the ones the white people had.

This was particularly true of the schools. The white power structure that controlled local and state governments in the South provided much less money to the black schools than to the ones their own children attended. This meant black schools could not hire as many teachers or buy as many books as the white schools were able to do. They could not even afford to keep up their buildings and grounds, and make them safe and comfortable. All this put African-American children at a terrible disadvantage. They were, in effect, denied their right to a good public education, and they were not prepared to compete equally for jobs when they got out of school. In a sense, they were almost as held down at the bottom of Southern society by the chains of segregation as they had once been bound by the real chains of slavery.

▶ The Court Speaks For The Constitution

The National Association for the Advancement of Colored People (NAACP) attacked Jim Crow laws by bringing a variety of cases into the federal courts. The most important were the cases that dealt with the segregation of public schools. One of these was the case of an African-American schoolgirl named Linda Brown. The NAACP went to court to object to the fact that Linda and other African-American children were forced to attend a segregated school in Topeka, Kansas.

The NAACP's best lawyer, a young African-American man named Thurgood Marshall, argued the *Brown* case before the Supreme Court. Education was a right in the United States, mandated by law, he argued. Refusing to give blacks and whites the same education violated the Constitution's guarantee of "equal protection" under the law. In a unanimous decision, all nine Justices agreed with Marshall and the NAACP. Separate schools, it declared, were "inherently unequal," and therefore unconstitutional. The South would have to desegregate—or integrate—its schools.

Brown did not end segregation in the South. It applied only to the public schools, and it would be many years before most southern schools complied with the ruling in any case. But *Brown* put an enormous crack in the wall of segregation, making it almost inevitable that the wall would eventually collapse. Over the next several years, the Supreme Court issued a series of opinions widening that crack. One by one, Jim Crow laws were struck down. State parks could no longer be segregated, ruled the Court. Neither could public beaches, or buses, or golf courses. In total, the Court was saying the black people had the same rights as white people to use public facilities in the United States.

The Supreme Court was demanding an enormous social change, and the white power

Thurgood Marshall argued the case of Brown *v.* Board of Education *before the Supreme Court. He later went on to become a Supreme Court Justice himself.*

structure resisted it. State governors in the South simply refused to integrate their public facilities. Mobs of white people gathered to keep black children from entering the white schools. They blocked the doors, yelled curses and racial insults at the children, and even threw rocks at them.

At the same time, the Ku Klux Klan (KKK) and other secret groups launched a campaign of violence and intimidation to terrorize African Americans and others who supported desegregation. Many white politicians secretly supported the Klan's efforts. The local police in many places refused to protect people from the Klan, much less to enforce the orders putting an end to Jim Crow laws themselves.

But the Supreme Court speaks for the Constitution—and the Constitution must be obeyed. In 1957, a reluctant President Dwight Eisenhower was forced to send combat-trained paratroopers to Little Rock, Arkansas, to protect nine black children who were trying to attend a previously all-white school. Eventually it became clear to everyone that the orders of the Supreme Court would have to be carried out.

▶ The Effects of *Brown*

Slowly, but unstoppably, the nation was forced to desegregate. The death of Jim Crow brought about an unprecedented transformation in American society. Before *Brown*, African Americans had little chance to succeed in American society. Only a relatively small proportion ever got any education beyond high school. Even in the North, they were usually confined to the lowest paying, most physical jobs.

Most of the handful who did manage to overcome the odds and become businesspeople, attorneys, doctors, or other professionals were forced to work only in black neighborhoods and deal only with black clients. In many parts of the country, black teachers could not teach white children. Black surgeons could not operate on white patients.

There is still discrimination in the United States. African Americans and other minorities are still at a disadvantage in many areas of American society. But—thanks to the Supreme Court—the races are no longer segregated by law. Black Americans now have many, though not yet all, of the same opportunities as white Americans have. And millions of them have seized those opportunities.

Today, African Americans work in virtually every field of American business, thousands as owners and executives. There are African-American doctors and surgeons on the staffs of virtually every large hospital in the country. There are African-American professors in almost every major university. There are African-American attorneys in the most prestigious law firms, and African-American judges in state and federal courts across the country. None of this would have been possible without *Brown* and the other desegregation orders of the U.S. Supreme Court.

The momentous changes brought about by *Brown* v. *Board of Education* and the other landmark decisions that followed it eventually transformed the

Supreme Court itself. For more than 170 years, only white Justices had sat on the Court. Then, in 1967, the first black Justice arrived. He was none other than Thurgood Marshall—the very attorney who had argued *Brown* v. *Board of Education* in front of the Court thirteen years before.

The U.S. Judicial System

The Supreme Court sits at the very top of the U.S. judicial system. Below it are a variety of "inferior"—or lower—courts. All these courts exist to resolve disputes.

Legal disputes arise between many different parties. They occur between individual people, between institutions, and between individuals and institutions. They even occur between individuals and the state. This is the case, for example, when a person is accused of a crime, which is considered an offense against the state.

In the American legal system, as in many other countries, legal disputes are often resolved through trials. These are adversarial contests between accusers and defendants. In civil cases, the accuser is known as the plaintiff. In criminal trials, it is the government that is the accuser, or prosecutor, who makes a charge against the defendant.

The trial is held in a court. The disputing parties (or attorneys working for them) present their evidence and make their arguments. In the end, it is up to either a judge or a jury who has listened to the case to decide which side will win.

Courts resolve disputes according to the laws—local, state, or federal—that apply to the case at hand. These laws are the rules by which American society operates. They define how people and institutions must behave in order for society to function smoothly and fairly.

▶ Kinds Of Cases

Courts deal with different kinds of cases by applying different kinds of laws. There are three main categories of cases and of laws: civil, criminal, and administrative.

Civil cases involve disputes between individuals or institutions. These disputes are brought to court in the form of lawsuits, in which a plaintiff sues a defendant. In the suit, the plaintiff claims to have suffered some damage because of the carelessness or misbehavior of the other party, called the defendant. The alleged damage can be either physical or purely financial, or, even both. The plaintiff might, for example, say that he or she was injured in an accident caused by the defendant, that he or she had had property destroyed, or that he or she had lost money because the defendant had been deliberately misleading about an investment. Whatever the alleged damage, in a civil case the plaintiff asks the court to order the defendant to pay money in compensation for the financial loss and the wrong suffered.

Criminal cases involve disputes between the state and individuals accused of crimes. Crimes are violations of criminal statutes. In most criminal cases, then, the dispute is between either a state government or the federal government and a defendant it accuses of committing a crime.

Administrative cases involve rules set by government agencies. A variety of state and federal agencies regulate certain kinds of business and professional dealings, as well as behavior that affects the environment and other activities that affect the public welfare. An administrative case arises when a government agency charges a defendant with disobeying a regulation, or when a private person or business argues that a government regulation is unfair or unreasonable.

▶ The Functions of Judges and Juries

Courts have three main jobs to do. First, they must determine the facts. That is, they must decide what actually happened. Did the defendant really do what he or she is accused of doing?

Second, the courts must decide how the law applies to the case. Did the defendant's action violate a criminal law, or did it unjustly wrong the civil plaintiff?

Third, the courts must decide what the consequence should be. If a civil wrong was committed, what does the defendant owe the plaintiff in compensation? If the defendant committed a crime, should the criminal go to jail? Be fined? Be put on probation?

Some courts have both a judge and a jury. Others have only a judge. Still others—including the U.S. Supreme Court—have several judges sitting together. In courts that have both a judge and a jury, the jury usually decides on the facts of the case, while the judge decides how the laws apply to it. When the court rules that a wrong has been done, either the judge or the jury may decide what the penalty should be.

The party that loses in a trial has the right to appeal the decision to another court. These so-called higher courts—known as appellate courts—do not have juries, and they do not usually hold actual trials. Instead, the judge or judges sitting on the court examine the record of what happened in the lower court to be sure that the party appealing the decision was given the "due process of law" guaranteed by the U.S. Constitution. In simple terms, "due process" means fairness. The court must be sure that all the laws applying to the case, as well as all the legal procedures involved, have been followed. In other words, the court must be sure that the trial was conducted fairly and that all the defendant's rights were protected.

▶ Local Courts

There are three main levels of courts in the United States. The lowest level is made up of local courts, such as county and municipal courts, traffic courts, justice's courts, magistrate's courts, and police courts. These courts deal mostly with traffic offenses and violations of local ordinances, as well as minor criminal charges.

The single judge who usually presides over a local court sometimes handles the opening stages of more serious criminal proceedings as well. Immediately following an arrest for a major criminal offense, or felony, the police court judge decides whether to set bail or send the defendant to jail until prosecutors prepare an indictment. The later stages of most felony cases, as well as most civil disputes, are usually handled by state courts.

▶ State Courts

Each state has its own court system, established under the constitution of that particular state. It has jurisdiction over most legal disputes that arise in the state, including disputes between citizens of different states. Since most criminal acts are violations of state laws, this includes the great majority of criminal cases. In fact, state courts hear the vast majority of all the legal cases in the United States.

In addition to the regular state courts, each state also has one or more higher courts that hear appeals. The highest court in most states is called the state Supreme Court. In New York and Maryland, however, it is known as the Court of Appeals.

▶ Federal Courts

In addition to the U.S. Supreme Court, the federal court system is made up of district courts, federal courts of appeals, and legislative courts.

District Courts. These are the trial courts of the federal system. A trial court is one which tries the facts and determines what happened. It determines whether or not a crime was actually committed, whether or not a civil wrong was actually done, or whether or not a defendant is guilty. Like the lower state courts, then, district courts hear the evidence and arguments in each case and make a decision.

Also, as in state courts, most federal trials are jury trials, presided over by a judge. In some constitutional cases, however, the right to a jury trial is waived, and the case is heard by a judge.

At least one district court is located in each state, as well as in the territories of Guam, Puerto Rico, and the Virgin Islands. The larger states have more than one. California and Texas, for example, each have four district courts. The total number of district courts can change. In 1993, there were ninety-four. Between them, these courts hear more than three-quarters of all federal cases brought each year.

A small district court, like the ones in Guam or the Virgin Islands, may have only one judge. Most have more, however. The Delaware district, for example, had two judges in 1993; Rhode Island had three. Some large districts have many more. The northern district of Illinois, for example, had twenty judges.

U.S. Courts of Appeals. Just as in state courts, the losing side in a federal court has the rightto appeal the decision. Originally, the U.S. Supreme Court heard all federal appeals, but there were so many of them by the late nineteenth century that the Court was overwhelmed. In 1891, Congress established a new level of courts, known as the U.S. Courts of Appeals, to take the pressure off the Supreme Court.

Today, there are thirteen courts of appeals spread around the country. One, known as the United States Court of Appeals for the Federal District, specializes in patent and customs cases. The others handle a wide variety of appeals. These include not only civil and criminal cases from the federal district courts, but also appeals from administrative decisions made by federal regulatory agencies. Because they are appeals courts, circuit courts do not have juries, and no facts can be brought into evidence. Their job is to determine if the lower courts did a fair job.

As can be gathered from the small number of circuit courts, most have jurisdiction over appeals from federal courts in several districts. The jurisdiction of a circuit court is determined by geography, although the geographic reach of the different circuits varies widely. The Seventh Circuit, for example, hears cases from the three neighboring states of Wisconsin, Illinois, and Indiana. The Ninth Circuit, on the other hand, hears cases from Alaska, Hawaii, Guam, and the Northern Mariana Islands, as well as seven western states.

Legislative Courts. The district and appeals courts are known as "constitutional courts" because they were established under Article III of the U.S. Constitution, which declares that "the judicial power of the United States shall be vested in one Supreme Court, and in such inferior courts as the Congress may from time to time ordain and establish." But Congress has also established a variety of "legislative courts" to deal with specific kinds of cases. These include: the U.S. Court of Federal Claims, or Court of Claims, which handles claims against the federal government; the U.S. Tax Court; the U.S. Court of International Trade; and the U.S. Court of Military Appeals.

While judges in other federal courts usually serve for life, judges in legislative courts have fixed terms.

▶ Jurisdiction

Not all courts can hear all cases. Each kind and level of court has its own jurisdiction. That is, it has the authority to hear certain kinds of cases, but not others. In general, local courts try cases involving local laws; state courts hear cases involving state laws; and federal courts hear cases involving federal laws.

The lower state courts and U.S. District Courts are the courts of original jurisdiction for most civil and criminal cases in the United States. That is, they are the courts that have the responsibility to decide them. As trial courts, they determine the facts of the case. The higher appeals courts (also known as appellate courts) only hear such cases on appeal. Their job is to rule on questions of law.

Some disputes can be brought to either the state or federal courts, because there are both state and federal laws that apply to them. Although state courts have jurisdiction over most civil cases, federal courts have jurisdiction in two instances. One is when a citizen of one state sues a citizen of another. Even then, however, the federal court takes jurisdiction only when an amount of money over $50,000 is at stake. The other instance is when significant questions of federal law are involved.

When two courts each have jurisdiction, the complaining party usually chooses where to bring the case. In criminal cases, the local, state, and federal prosecutors must decide among themselves at which level to bring the indictment. Although federal prosecutors have greater authority, most criminal cases are brought in state courts. In civil cases, the plaintiff's attorney usually looks at both the state and federal laws that apply, and then decides which set of laws will be most favorable. He or she then brings the case to that court system.

▶ The U.S. Supreme Court

The Constitution gives the U.S. Supreme Court original jurisdiction over "all Cases affecting Ambassadors, other public Ministers and Consuls, and those in which a State shall be a Party." If this was all the Supreme Court had to do, however, it would not be very busy. The Court almost never hears more than five original jurisdiction cases a year.[1] Most of those are disputes between states.

But the Supreme Court has another role as well, a role that keeps it much busier than its limited role as a trial court. It is, in fact, the highest appellate court in the land, and the one with the broadest jurisdiction. It hears appeals, not only from the U.S.

The Supreme Court building in Washington, D.C. houses the highest appeals court in the land. It is the most powerful court in the world.

District Courts, the U.S. Courts of Appeals, the federal legislative courts, and a variety of federal agencies, but from every state court system in the nation as well.

As the highest appeals court in the land, it can overrule any and all of these other courts and agencies. As the final guardian of the U.S. Constitution, it can under certain circumstances overturn laws passed by the U.S. Congress, and tell the President of the United States what to do. This ability to give orders to the government of the most economically and militarily powerful nation on Earth makes the Supreme Court the most powerful court in the world.

It was not always that way, however, as we shall see in the next chapter.

The Court Invents Itself

The Constitution established a Supreme Court for the United States of America, but it said almost nothing about what that Court should do. The Court would have to invent itself as it went along. As it turned out, it would take several generations of Justices—and two centuries of history—to make the Court what it is today.

▶ False Start

Despite its grand title, the Supreme Court did not start out as the powerful branch of government it has become. In fact, it began as a fairly small and modest institution. Its role was limited to hearing appeals from "inferior courts," and deciding cases in which "ambassadors, public ministers [or] consuls" or state governments were parties. During the early years of the Court's existence, this meant that it had practically no role at all.

The first meeting of the Supreme Court took place February 2, 1790. It was held in the Royal Exchange building in New York City, which had been named the nation's capital the year before. The Court had actually been scheduled to meet on the first of February, but half of the Justices were unable to make it to New York in time. When they finally got together, they had no cases to hear, so they went home. It would be three years before they would decide their first case.[1]

The first meeting of the Supreme Court, in 1790, was held in the Royal Exchange building in New York City.

▶ An "Intolerable" Job

The Constitution was so vague about the Supreme Court that it did not even say how many members the Court should have. Congress originally set the size of the Court at six, made up of five Associate Justices and one Chief Justice. Six was chosen because there were six federal circuit courts at that time. In 1801, the size of the Supreme Court was cut by one Justice, only to be increased again to six the next year. For awhile after that, whenever Congress added a new circuit, it added a new Justice to the Supreme Court as well.

The number of Justices swelled to ten at the time of the Civil War, but during Reconstruction, Congress moved to prevent President Andrew Johnson from appointing new members by decreeing that Justices who died or retired should not be replaced. The number of Justices had shrunk to seven by 1869, when Congress reset it permanently at nine.

To put it mildly, a seat on the Court was not highly prized in the early days. To the statesmen and politicians of the late eighteenth century, it seemed like a thankless, dead-end job. The Court was far and away the weakest branch of government, and there was little prospect for its power to expand. The Constitution left it up to Congress, not the Court, to make whatever "regulations" it wanted to make for the Court, and it was unlikely to give the Justices more power in the future.

Not surprisingly, President George Washington had trouble coming up with six distinguished men willing to fill the seats. The celebrated statesman John Jay did agree to become the first Chief Justice, but he soon declared the post "intolerable."[2] As Chief Justice, Jay presided over meetings of the Court, but had no more real power to decide cases than any of the other members of the Court. Each Justice's vote counted the same, and the decisions they made hardly seemed to matter very much anyway. Altogether, Jay found the Court short on "energy, weight and dignity,"[3] and wanted out as soon as possible.

Eager to escape the Court, Jay ran for governor of New York in 1792. When he lost, he agreed to stay on the Court until the next state election, in 1794, when he ran again. This time he won, and happily resigned as Chief Justice to become governor of New York.

The Court had moved to Philadelphia in 1791, when the "City of Brotherly Love" was named the nation's new capital. In 1800, it moved again, to the permanent capital city of Washington, D.C. But the changes of scenery did little to improve either the status or power of the Court. It would take a bold decision—announced by a new Chief Justice—to give the Court the energy, weight, and dignity it lacked.

▶ The Court Says "What the Law Is"

President John Adams lost the election of 1800 to Thomas Jefferson. Adams and Jefferson were long-time rivals who headed opposing political factions. Before turning over the government to his old adversary, Adams wanted to get as many of his supporters

Statesman John Jay was the first Chief Justice of the Supreme Court. He declared the post "intolerable."

into federal office as possible. Once there, they could cause trouble for the incoming administration.

In the last days of his presidency, Adams had Secretary of State John Marshall draw up commissioning papers awarding judgeships to forty-two of his fellow Federalists. Unfortunately for Adams, four of those papers had not been delivered by the time Jefferson was inaugurated. The new President refused to deliver them. He wanted to name his own judges. William Marbury and three other Adams appointees sued Jefferson's secretary of State, James Madison, demanding to be made judges.

The case was more a political battle than a legal one. By the time the suit was brought, John Marshall—the Adams man who had drawn up the papers in the first place—had become the fourth Chief Justice of the Supreme Court. James Madison refused to even appear before the Court to answer the suit, and the worried Jeffersonians in Congress actually cancelled the 1802 term of the Supreme Court to keep it from ruling in the case.

The Court was determined to decide the issue, however, and the Jeffersonians could not stall forever. In February 1803, the Court finally handed down its decision—a decision that would astound the nation and establish a momentous new role for the Supreme Court.

Speaking for the entire Court, Marshall denied the suit. Marbury had asked the Court to issue a "writ of mandamus" to James Madison—that is, an order commanding him to instate the judges Adams had appointed. But Marshall declared that the Court could not do this. Why not? Because the law Congress had passed giving the Court the power to issue a writ of mandamus was unconstitutional.

In theory, the Court was ruling in favor of Madison, Jefferson, and the executive branch of government. They did not have to make Marbury a judge. But in reality, the Supreme Court was ruling in favor of itself. It was giving itself an immense new power—a power that neither Congress nor the executive branch had ever granted that the Court should have! This was the power to accept or reject the laws written by Congress.

"It is emphatically the province and duty of the judicial department to say what the law is," Marshall declared in his historic opinion. And, "If two laws conflict with each other, the courts must decide on the operation of each." What's more, since "the Constitution is superior to any ordinary act of the legislature," the Court has the power to review the laws passed by Congress and to strike them down if the Court decides they conflict with the Constitution.[4]

This was not a new idea. It had even been suggested by Alexander Hamilton in "Federalist 78," one of the written arguments published by supporters of the Constitution during the debate over whether to ratify it. But the Court had never invoked it before.

This power, first legally established in *Marbury* v. *Madison*, is known as the power of judicial review.

It forms the basis for many of the most important decisions the Supreme Court makes. It is also the basis of many attacks on the Court by critics who accuse it of abusing this power. They charge that the Court sometimes goes beyond interpreting the laws written by the legislatures, and makes up new laws of its own.

▶ Marshall Strengthens the Court

John Marshall, who served on the Court from 1801 to 1835, was the first great Chief Justice, and probably the most important of them all. Besides greatly expanding the Court's power in *Marbury*, Marshall worked to strengthen the institution from the inside. Under him, the Court went far toward establishing a major place for itself in the government of the United States.

Before Marshall, each Justice wrote a separate, or seriatim, opinion on each case. Each spoke for himself, and no one spoke for the Court. Even when most—or all—of the Justices agreed which side should win, each gave his own reasons why. This tended to be confusing for people trying to figure out what the decision really meant, and to predict what the Court might do in the future.

Marshall persuaded his colleagues to join in a single, majority opinion stating the reasons for the Court's decision. Individual Justices who disagreed could still issue separate opinions, but the majority opinion would speak for the Court itself. This allowed the Court to speak with a single, strong voice that carried a new weight of authority.

John Marshall is remembered as the first great Chief Justice. He served on the Court from 1801 to 1835.

That voice was often the voice of Marshall himself. He wrote 519 of the 1,106 majority opinions the Court issued while he was Chief Justice.[5] A devoted Federalist, Marshall's opinions helped to strengthen, as well as to define, the power of the federal government of the young Republic.

▶ Upholding the Public Interest

Like Marshall, the man who followed him as Chief Justice would have an enormous impact on the reputation of the Court. Unfortunately, that impact would be almost as negative as Marshall's was positive.

Roger Taney (1836–1854) was appointed by Andrew Jackson, the President of "the common man." As Chief Justice, he upheld the interests of the public over those of wealthy and powerful individuals or businesses. His majority decision in the case of the *Charles River Bridge Company*[6] established the principle that "The object and end of all government is to promote the happiness and prosperity of the community." Although "the rights of private property must be sacredly guarded," Taney wrote, "we must not forget that the community also have rights. . . ." This was an important principle, and one that helped form the basis for the regulatory power of government.

Many legal scholars consider Taney one of the greatest of all the Justices who ever sat on the Court. His historical reputation was seriously damaged, however, by the decision he wrote for the Court in *Dred Scott* v. *John F. A. Sandford*, better known as the Dred Scott case. This infamous decision will be

Chief Justice Roger Taney was appointed by President Andrew Jackson. Many scholars consider Taney one of the greatest of all the Justices to sit on the Court.

discussed in a later chapter dealing with momentous Court decisions.

▶ "The One Place in Government I Would Have Liked to Fill Myself"

In 1789, John Jay had felt so insignificant as Chief Justice that he abandoned the post to become governor of New York. By 1910, however, the job had grown so desirable that William Howard Taft preferred it to his own job as President of the United States. Forced to appoint a new Chief Justice, he chose Edward D. White, but complained that "the one place in the government which I would have liked to fill myself I am forced to give to another."[7] Taft eventually got his wish in 1921, when President Warren G. Harding appointed him—now an ex-President—to the post.

Taft was a spirited Chief Justice (1921–1930) who was much happier on the Court than he had been as President. More than anyone else, he helped to organize and streamline the Court for the twentieth century. Before him, the Court had to take many cases whether it wanted to or not. It was in danger of becoming so snowed under with cases that it couldn't function. Taft used his highly developed political skills and contacts to coax Congress into passing the Judiciary Act of 1925, which gave the Court more right to pick and choose its cases. The Act reduced the mandatory jurisdiction of the Court, and allowed it to refer many cases it had once had to hear itself to the federal courts of appeals.

Chief Justice William Howard Taft was once President of the United States. Of the two positions, he preferred his post on the Court.

▶ Two Great Justices

Taft was an excellent Chief Justice in many ways. In the eyes of most legal scholars, however, he was overshadowed by two Associate Justices who served with him: Oliver Wendell Holmes and Louis Brandeis. They are ranked with the likes of John Marshall as among the handful of truly great Supreme Court Justices ever to sit on the Court.

Both Holmes and Brandeis were already on the Court when Taft arrived, and both would remain there after he died. Holmes had been nominated by Theodore Roosevelt in 1902 and served until 1932. He was the son of the writer and doctor, Oliver Wendell Holmes, Sr., of Boston. Oliver, Jr., trained as an attorney and became a teacher and writer on legal matters. He argued that the law was a response to changing social conditions, and not just a collection of lifeless rules and old traditions.

As a practical matter, Holmes believed that the law should be used to protect people against careless or intentional injuries. A collection of his lectures, published as *The Common Law* in 1881, made his views known not only in the United States but in Europe as well. It has had a great effect on the way judges have looked at the law ever since.

Holmes wrote more majority opinions for the Supreme Court than any other Justice before or since, but he is best known for his powerful dissents. He particularly objected to the Court majority's habit of striking down progressive social measures passed by legislatures. Despite being quite

Justice Oliver Wendell Holmes wrote more majority opinions for the Court than any other Justice before or since. Yet, he is better known for his powerful dissents.

conservative himself, he believed the Court should respect the will of the people, as expressed by the people's elected representatives. He was so persuasive in disagreement that he earned the nickname the Great Dissenter.

Louis Brandeis was also known for his eloquent dissents, although, like Holmes, he wrote more majority opinions than dissents. Born and raised in Kentucky, Brandeis made a name for himself practicing law in Boston. In his early career, he was both a brilliant business attorney and a liberal reformer. Although he made a fortune working in private practice for wealthy clients, he also worked for free on cases he believed to be in the public interest. This work earned him the reputation of being the "people's attorney."

In 1908, he presented a unique legal brief in favor of an Oregon law limiting the workday of women to ten hours. Most legal briefs at the time were devoted largely to quoting laws and earlier Court decisions, but Brandeis hardly bothered with those. Instead, he asked the Court to consider the effects of the law on actual people. Most of his historic brief was made up of statistics and scholarly studies showing the harmful effect of longer workdays on women. He won the case. When other attorneys began following his example, such sociological legal arguments became famous as "Brandeis briefs."

Nominated to the Supreme Court by Woodrow Wilson in 1916, Brandeis was the first Jew to serve as a Justice. This was considered a progressive step because there was a great deal of anti-Semitism in the country at that time. Brandeis was also by far the most liberal member of the Court during that time. That is, he supported reform and social experimentation, unlike more conservative members of the Court who were tied to tradition and hostile to change. What's more, he was more concerned with the welfare of individuals than with the rights of property and businesses.

Brandeis was a staunch defender of personal liberties, which he believed went beyond the rights specifically mentioned in the Constitution. He argued, for example, that the Fourth Amendment freedom from unreasonable search and seizure implied a right of privacy. He described this as "the right to be let alone—the most comprehensive of rights and the right most valued by civilized men."[8] As early as 1920, he suggested that the fundamental freedoms guaranteed by the Bill of Rights might be applied to the states.

The moderate Charles Evans Hughes took over as Chief Justice in 1930, just as the country was about to sink into the Great Depression. When the liberal Democratic President Franklin D. Roosevelt launched the economic reforms of the New Deal in 1932, the Court's conservative majority resisted. They thought Roosevelt's policies too radical, and declared several of the President's measures unconstitutional. Although Brandeis disliked some of them himself, he voted to uphold most of them and became recognized as the New Deal's leading defender on the Court. Like Holmes, he believed that the Court should bow to Congress and the President on economic matters.

The Court became increasingly liberal as the 1930s went on and President Roosevelt was able to appoint more Justices. By the time Brandeis was ready to leave the Court in 1939, he was leading a progressive majority. By then, many of his old dissenting positions—on such matters as the Bill of Rights and social legislation—had become the accepted opinions of the Court.

▶ Judicial "Liberals" and "Conservatives"

People speak of politicians as being either conservative or liberal, and they speak of Supreme Court Justices in the same way. Judicial "conservatives" tend to argue for judicial restraint. They believe that judges should not apply laws in ways that go beyond the intent of the legislators who wrote them.

When it comes to the Constitution, judicial conservatives tend to be strict constructionists. That is, they interpret—or construe—the Constitution to mean exactly what its words say, and nothing more. They object when more liberal Justices "read into" the Constitution protections that are not specifically spelled out there. They scoff at the idea that there might be a Constitutional right to "privacy," for instance, because the Constitution doesn't mention the word "privacy."

Judicial liberals, on the other hand, believe that

the Constitution is a living document. They argue that different historical circumstances call for different interpretations of its words. They point out that many of its provisions—and particularly of the early amendments known as the Bill of Rights—are written broadly. This, they say, allows them to be interpreted in new ways by new generations, facing new national and legal problems. Liberals, then, tend to be judicial activists who interpret the laws in ways which expand the rights granted in the Constitution, and extend them to new groups of people.

The distinctions between judicial liberals and conservatives are not always clear cut, however. Nor do they always reflect the politically liberal or conservative views of the Justice. Political conservatives can sometimes be judicial activists, re-interpreting or striking down laws they consider too liberal. The politically and judicially liberal Louis Brandeis, on the other hand, argued for judicial restraint in defending the reform legislation of the New Deal. He did not believe that the conservative Courts should undermine the will of the people, as expressed in the liberal laws passed by their representatives in Congress.

▶ The Court Moves Toward Conservatism

Under Chief Justice Earl Warren (1953–1969), the Court became more liberal, in both senses of the word, than ever before. The Warren Court issued a wide range of monumental decisions that had the effect of greatly expanding the civil rights of individuals. It broadened the protections given to people accused of crimes, and limited the powers of the police; it required the states to redraw election districts to assure "one man, one vote;" and it established the constitutional right to privacy Brandeis had argued for decades earlier. Most important, in *Brown* v. *Board of Education*, it struck down racial segregation of the schools, and paved the way for the end of Jim Crow.

There tends to be a long ebb and flow to the direction of the Supreme Court, however. A move in a liberal direction is often followed by a swing back toward conservatism, and vice versa. This swing occurred again in the 1970s and 1980s, as Republican Presidents appointed more and more conservative Justices, who gradually began to undo some of what the Warren Court had done.

The process started under Chief Justice Warren Burger (1969–1986), who was appointed by the Republican President Richard Nixon. By the early 1980s, it was clear that the Court was becoming less concerned with the rights of people accused of crimes, for instance, and more sympathetic with the tactics of police and prosecutors. Unlike the Warren Court, the Burger Court was not eager to put new restrictions on the ability of law enforcement officials to arrest, hold, and coerce suspects. If anything, it was inclined to loosen such restrictions and make it easier for the police to catch criminals, and for prosecutors to convict them.

Although the Court tends to be more or less liberal or conservative at different times, it is rarely absolutely one or the other. The Burger Court pleased many liberals by continuing to enforce racial integration through school busing, and, in the case of *Roe* v. *Wade*, striking down state laws against abortion and thus establishing a positive constitutional right to abortion.[9]

What's more, it even ruled unanimously against President Nixon when he refused to let Congress hear tapes he had made in the White House that might incriminate him in the Watergate Scandal. In a decision written by Nixon's own appointee,

Under Chief Justice Earl Warren (seated, center) the Court became more liberal. Shown here are the members of the Supreme Court during its 1954 session.

Warren Burger, the Court ordered the President to produce the tapes. He did, and they proved as incriminating as the President had feared. Nixon was forced to resign from office soon after the tapes were disclosed.

On the important issue of capital punishment—which liberals tend to oppose and conservatives to favor—the Burger Court seemed to veer both ways. In *Furman* v. *Georgia*[10] in 1972, it found the death penalty unconstitutional. Convinced that the states were so inconsistent and racially unfair in the way they chose which criminals to execute, the Justices ruled that capital punishment as then carried out had become "cruel and unusual punishment." All executions were stopped in the United States, and most people assumed they would never start up again.

But several states quickly wrote new capital punishment laws that they hoped the Court would accept. Four years later, in 1976, the Court found Georgia's new law constitutional in the case known as *Gregg* v. *Georgia*,[11] and executions resumed in many states. Even then, however, the Court insisted on a variety of safeguards against the possibility of unjust executions, and made it relatively easy for condemned people to appeal their death sentences.

The Court has become much more conservative under its current Chief Justice, William Rehnquist. Rehnquist was appointed to the Court by President Nixon in 1972 and raised to Chief Justice by President Ronald Reagan in 1986. The Rehnquist

Under Chief Justice William Rehnquist, the Supreme Court became more conservative.

Court has been less inclined to use its powers to enforce racial equality than any Court since *Brown*. It has been even more tolerant of police tactics than the Burger Court, and it has been positively hostile to death penalty appeals. It has drastically "streamlined" the process for those appeals, and has made it very hard for a condemned person to make more than one appeal to the federal courts. In 1992, it directly ordered federal judges in California to stop granting delays of the execution of the killer Robert Alton Harris, no matter what their legal reason— something no Supreme Court had ever done before.

▶ Women on the Court

The first 112 Supreme Court Justices were all men. For most of the United States' history, it was simply taken for granted that attorneys and judges—not to mention Supreme Court Justices—would be men. Even after women started joining the bar in increasing numbers in the mid-twentieth century, it was still assumed that the best legal minds belonged to men. It seemed only natural, then, for only men to be nominated to the Supreme Court. The prejudice against women was so strong that even liberal Justices were reluctant to hire women as clerks. In 1960, a top law school graduate named Ruth Bader Ginsburg applied for a clerkship with the legendary liberal, Justice Felix Frankfurter. He turned her down with the declaration that he was not ready for a woman.[12]

It was not until 1981 that President Ronald Reagan appointed the first woman, Sandra Day

Justice Sandra Day O'Connor was the first woman appointed to the Supreme Court, in 1981. Since then, a second woman, Ruth Bader Ginsburg, has joined her.

O'Connor, to the Court. O'Connor was a graduate of Stanford Law School who had gone into politics in Arizona before becoming a state court judge in 1974. Generally a conservative, like the President who appointed her, she has been an influential force in decisions limiting affirmative action, abortion rights, and government entanglement in religion.

In 1993, President Bill Clinton nominated another woman to sit on the Court. His choice was a New York attorney who had been very active in expanding the legal rights and opportunities of women. She was none other than Ruth Bader Ginsburg, whom Justice Frankfurter had once turned down even for a clerkship, because she was a woman.

▶ A Check and a Balance

The powers and responsibilities of the Supreme Court have grown enormously since the Justices adjourned their first session because they had nothing to do. In the two centuries that have passed since, the Court has become a worthy partner of the executive and legislative branches, and a key element in the system of checks and balances that keeps our government on track.

How the Court Works

The Supreme Court is the smallest of the three great institutions of the federal government. Its entire staff consists of less than four hundred people, compared to the nearly thirty-six thousand who work for the legislative branch, and the nearly three million who work for the executive branch.[1]

Among other duties, this relatively small staff runs the Court's many offices; handles the deluge of petitions, court records, and other documents that flood the Court; maintains the Court's library; keeps the Court's records; provides security; and informs lower courts, and the public at large, about the Court's activities. The most important staff members are the law clerks, who assist the Justices, and the five staff officers who supervise the various departments of the Court's offices.

▶ The Law Clerks

Each Justice is entitled to have four clerks, or personal assistants. Most Justices use all four, although some make do with fewer. Chief Justice William Rehnquist, for example, has only three. Individual clerks usually serve for one year.

Justices are free to choose their clerks in any way they want. Most pick recent top graduates from such major law schools as Yale, Harvard, and Stanford, many of whom have already clerked in lower federal courts. There is no shortage of applicants. A Supreme Court clerkship is one of the most prestigious positions a law graduate can obtain, and hundreds of eager applicants apply to each Justice every year.

Law clerks do much of the detailed legal work the Justices have no time for. They act as gatekeepers, reading the petitions that flood into the Court and summarizing the longer or more interesting ones for the Justices. Because of this, clerks sometimes have a strong influence on which cases get heard by the Court.

Once the Court has decided to consider a case, clerks do much of the legal research for their Justices. A clerk is often more familiar with the details of a case than the Justice, and Justices often rely heavily on their advice. It is believed that some Justices even let trusted clerks prepare opinions for them, doing little more than making a few changes or corrections themselves.

Some people think the clerks have far too much power. "Basically, you have 25-year-olds creating constitutional law," one critic complained. "They're doing what the Justices are supposed to be doing."[2] Despite such suspicions, the true responsibility for the final decision in a case always rests with the Justices, not the clerks.

▶ Officers of the Court

The working offices of the Court are divided into several departments. The Legal Office is staffed by two attorneys, who prepare memoranda regarding motions for the Court and handle the Court's own legal affairs.

The clerk heads up the department that runs the day-to-day affairs of the Court. His or her office handles the flow of paperwork, keeps the Court's schedule, maintains its records, and advises outside attorneys and others with business before the Court. The clerk also processes several thousand requests each year from attorneys wanting to be admitted to the Supreme Court bar. This is a necessary step before they can be permitted to argue a case before the Supreme Court.

The administrative assistant to the Chief Justice helps him (and presumably someday, her) fulfill his many administrative duties as head of the Court.

The reporter of decisions sees to it that the Court's opinions are in proper format, and that they are printed and published in the *United States Reports.*

The public information officer deals with the press and others interested in the workings of the Court.

The librarian oversees the Court's half-million volume library, while the curator maintains the Court's important collection of historical documents and other materials.

By far the largest domain belongs to the marshal, who oversees the more than two hundred men and women who provide security and maintain the physical plant of the Supreme Court building and grounds.

The newest of the Court's offices belongs to the director of data systems, who supervises the Court's electronic word and data-processing systems. Unlike the law clerks, these officers and the people who work under them are long-term employees.

▶ How Cases Come to the Court

The vast majority of cases that reach the Supreme Court come as petitions asking the Court to review a decision of a federal district court or state appeals court. Many of these petitions are filed by experienced attorneys, and some even by state attorney generals. But not all of them are. You do not have to be a high-powered attorney to appeal to the Supreme Court. You do not even have to be a lawyer at all. Any citizen who feels that she or he has been denied justice in the lower courts can ask the Supreme Court to hear their case.

Why would anyone file a petition with the Supreme Court without a lawyer? For one thing, filing a petition with the Supreme Court can cost a lot of money. Attorneys are extremely expensive, and there are fees to pay. But petitioners who cannot afford these expenses can avoid these fees and file their own case *in forma pauperis*, with or without an attorney.

Many do. In fact, the majority of petitions the Court receives are so-called "pauper petitions."[3] Many come from convicted criminals who believe they have been unjustly convicted. Some are little more than misspelled scribbling, penned in their prison cells by desperate convicts with no other hope for freedom.

Most of these "pauper petitions" are rejected—as are most of the expertly prepared legal briefs filed by high-priced attorneys who are used to doing business before the Supreme Court. But all are read and considered for a hearing, and each year several of these "pauper cases" result in Supreme Court decisions.

By far the most famous of these was a handprinted petition from a prison inmate who signed himself "Clarence Earl Gideon." Gideon had been convicted of breaking and entering a Florida poolroom. Because he could not afford an attorney, he had been forced to defend himself at his trial. He was now asking the Supreme Court to overturn his conviction on the grounds that his right to a fair trial had been denied because he had no lawyer to defend him. The Court appointed an experienced Washington attorney, Abe Fortas, to present Gideon's appeal.[4]

In a unanimous decision, the Justices agreed with Gideon and overturned his conviction. It was this case—which came to the Court scrawled on prison stationery—that established the Constitutional right of every criminal defendant in serious cases, no matter how poor they may be, to have an attorney.

▶ Granting "Cert"

The Court used to be required by law to hear all appeals from any decision of a federal district court or a state appeals court that a disputant wanted to bring to it. By the early twentieth century, however, the Court was so overwhelmed by such appeals that it could hardly function.

Pressed by Chief Justice William Howard Taft, Congress came to the overworked Justices' rescue with the Judiciary Act of 1925, which gave the Justices the freedom to refuse to hear most appeals they did not consider important. This left the Court with only a handful of cases it was strictly required to hear, and the Judicial Improvements and Access to Justice Act of 1988 removed virtually all of those. The Justices are now virtually free to control their own workload and to choose which cases they want to decide.

When the Court does decides to hear a case, it grants the petitioner a writ of certiorari (sur-she-'rere). This is an order from the Court, asking the lower courts to send it the record of the case in dispute. The Rules of the Supreme Court declare that "cert" (as it is known for short) "will be granted only when there are special and important reasons therefor."[5]

Parties to disputes know that the Supreme Court is extremely picky about which cases it will hear, and so the vast majority of potential cases are never submitted to the Court at all. Even so, many more petitions pour into the Court than the busy Justices can possibly hear, and they continue to refuse most of them. In fact, they seem to be getting more selective all the time. Today they typically "grant cert" in roughly 125 cases each term—less than 2 percent of the 6,000 to 7,000 petitions they receive.

Because so many petitions flood the Court, the Justices do not have time to read them all. Instead, the petitions are divided up among the clerks. Each clerk summarizes those he or she is responsible for, pointing out the key issues involved. These memos are sent to the Justices to use in considering if they would like to hear the case. All but one of the current Justices participates in this so-called "cert pool."

The Justices then hold a conference to decide together which cases to hear. This meeting is held in strict privacy, and the vote totals are not announced to the public. Most of the petitions are not even voted on, in fact, since no Justice considers them worthy of a hearing. Others are discussed, and sometimes even argued. Then a vote is taken. If four of the nine Justices vote to consider a case, certiorari is granted. If not, it is denied.

When the Court refuses to "grant cert," the decision of the lower court is allowed to stand. This does not necessarily mean that the Justices agree with the lower court's decision, however. Since they have not decided the legal issue involved, the Court takes no position either way. Unfortunately, this is no help to the petitioner, since the denial of certiorari has the same effect on the case in question that denying the appeal would have had.

Although the great majority of cases reach the

The Justices meet privately in a conference room such as this to decide together which cases will be heard.

Court by way of a writ of certiorari, some are appealed directly from three-judge district court cases. These are usually cases that concern such matters as voting rights and federal redistricting.

▶ Oral Arguments

Once the Court decides to hear a case, it sends for the records from the lower courts. A schedule is set for the attorneys on both sides to submit written briefs presenting their arguments to the Court. The Justices decide whether to allow the attorneys to appear before the Court to make their arguments orally, or to rely on the written briefs the two sides will submit.[6]

On days when oral arguments are scheduled, the Justices meet in the conference room. By long custom, they all shake hands with each other before entering the great courtroom from behind a large red velvet curtain. They take their assigned places at the nine chairs behind the raised, angled bench that extends along one end of the room. The Chief Justice sits in the center, with the other Justices arranged according to the length of time they have served on the Court. The longest-serving Justice sits to the Chief

On days when oral arguments are scheduled, the Justices take their assigned places at the nine chairs behind the bench in the great courtroom.

Justice's right, the next longest to his left, and so on, back and forth.

From their exalted positions, high on the bench, they look down on the attorneys seated at tables below them. On one of these tables is a podium with microphones, where the lawyer with permission to speak stands when addressing the Justices.

Every courtroom is a battleground, a place where two sides meet in combat, each striving to defeat the other. Great issues are often at stake. The rights, freedoms—and sometimes even the lives—of human beings often hang in the balance. And the courtroom of the Supreme Court is the greatest legal battleground of all. It is the field on which the final and most decisive battles in America's legal wars are fought.

The attorneys are the foot soldiers in these wars. Like real soldiers, they often come into combat both excited and terrified. It is intimidating to face the nine most important judges in the country, fighting perhaps the most important legal battle of your life. This is particularly true for newcomers, the raw recruits meeting on the legal battleground of the Supreme Court for the first time. Throats dry up. Knees get weak. Voices crack.

Sometimes, Justices try to help. Occasionally, as Justice Harry Blackmun once said, "things get so very tense that it's a good idea to either change the subject or to throw some wisecrack into the proceedings."[7] In one case, an attorney compared the opposing lawyer to the character Tweedledum in

Alice in Wonderland, who insisted that words meant something different than what they really said. "That didn't fool Alice," declared the attorney, "and I doubt very much that it will fool this Court." "Don't overestimate us," cracked Chief Justice William Rehnquist.[8]

The time allowed for oral arguments is strictly controlled. One half-hour is usually allowed to each side. That is not much time, but it is all the time each lawyer has to present a case, respond to their opponent's arguments, and to answer questions from the Justices. A big round clock hangs behind the head of the Chief Justice, a constant reminder to the attorneys that time is running out on them.

Court watchers pay close attention to the questions the Justices ask, searching for clues as to which way each Justice is leaning in the case. Some questions are openly hostile to a particular attorney's argument.

Justice Hugo Black was a staunch defender of freedom of the press. He became positively sarcastic when one attorney suggested that a law should be passed to muzzle the press under certain circumstances. The First Amendment provides that "Congress shall make no law . . . abridging freedom of the press," Black pointed out. "And you can read that to mean Congress may make 'some law' abridging freedom of the press?"[9]

Other questions are obviously friendly. A sympathetic Justice might actually raise a good argument the attorney had neglected to mention. Still other questions seem honestly puzzled, showing that the Justices are struggling to understand the issue involved.

Some Justices almost never ask questions. Others press the attorneys hard, forcing them to defend their positions. In recent years, Chief Justice William Rehnquist has gotten impatient with some of the newer Justices who take so much time asking questions that the attorneys have not had time to make their arguments.

When the red light on the podium signals that time has expired, the attorney who is speaking must stop. If answering a question posed by a Justice, however, the attorney may finish the answer. Occasionally, when the Justices are unsatisfied, or are caught up in a particular discussion, they give an attorney a little extra time. But this is rare. Most often, as soon as the allotted time is up, the Chief Justice briskly thanks the attorneys and calls the next case.

▶ Reaching Judgment

The Justices announce their decisions publicly, but they arrive at them in private. They meet on Wednesdays and Fridays to discuss the cases that have been argued before them, gathering together around a rectangular table in front of a fireplace on one side of a large room. They deliberate, and ultimately vote alone, without aides or even secretaries to take notes for them.

Most Justices treasure their privacy, but that is not the only reason for the secrecy in which they meet. They believe that it is the final decisions that are important, not the steps along the way. They do not want lower courts, or the public, distracted by reports of differences of opinion during the conferences.

This secrecy shields the details of Court deliberations, although from what some Justices have said publicly, it seems that they are usually courteous and reserved with each other. Emotions do sometimes break through, however, when there is strong disagreement over controversial cases.

After they have discussed a case, the Justices vote on it. Since there are nine Justices, there is usually a majority for one side or the other. When the Chief Justice is in the majority, he or she picks someone from the winning side to write the majority opinion. When the Chief Justice is not in the majority, the longest-serving Justice on the winning side decides who will write the opinion. This is an important decision because the majority opinion becomes, in effect, the law of the land.

It can be a great honor to write the majority opinion in an important case, but it is also a great burden. Justices often become known to history by the majority opinions they write. Chief Justice Earl Warren will always be best remembered as the man who wrote the decision that desegregated America's schools. Although Chief Justice Taney accomplished many great things while on the Court, he has become infamous for the disastrous decision he wrote refusing to free the slave, Dred Scott.

Justices often agree on which way a case should

be decided without agreeing on the reasons why that decision is reached. Justices who vote in the majority, but disagree with parts of the majority opinion, can explain the reasons for their votes in separate concurring (agreeing) opinions. Justices who vote against the majority can also explain their reasons in separate opinions known as dissents.

Both concurring and dissenting opinions can blur the message the Court is sending with its decisions. They emphasize disagreements among the Justices, and suggest that not all similar cases will be decided in the same way. Sometimes this confusion is inevitable because there are fundamental disagreements among the Justices that cannot be compromised. But, whenever possible, the Court likes to speak with a single voice, so that what it is saying will be unmistakably clear. The votes that are taken in the Wednesday and Friday conferences are not binding. Justices can change their minds, and sometimes do. Justices frequently lobby each other, coaxing their colleagues to change their mind. Those who write opinions try to word them in ways that other Justices will agree with. Drafts of opinions on both sides are passed around in hopes that they will persuade others to join them. Compromises are sometimes worked to convince shaky Justices to switch their vote.

The Justices take several things into account in making their decision. First, of course, they consider the facts of the case—the details of the dispute they have to decide. Then they consider the laws that apply. These include not only state and federal laws, but the U.S. Constitution itself. In deciding how these laws apply to the current case, the Justices examine how the Supreme Court and lower courts have decided similar cases in the past. These earlier decisions, known as precedents, help define what the law is.

Most of the time the Justices try to make their decision consistent with the legal precedents. Occasionally, however, the Justices decide that the courts—including earlier Supreme Courts—were wrong. It overturns the precedents, reverses the earlier court decisions, and sets the law on a new course. This is what the Court did in *Brown* v. *Board of Education*, for example, when it overturned the legal precedents upholding racial segregation in the schools.

▶ Announcing the Decision

Decisions are formally announced from the bench, in the same courtroom where the Justices hear oral arguments. Even before the announcement, the reporter of decision's office has printed not only the majority opinion but all the concurring and dissenting opinions as well.

Most actual announcements are short and to the point. A Justice who has written an opinion appears in the courtroom, seated at the bench with the other Justices. He or she briefly describes what the case is about, and reports the Court's decision. Meanwhile the clerk presents the opinion, in writing, to the attorneys on all sides. Others interested in the case, including reporters, can get copies of the opinions from the Public Information Office.

At one time, all the Justices read their opinions, concurring and dissenting alike, aloud from the bench. Since opinions often run for scores of pages, this could sometimes take a very long time, and so the practice has been largely abandoned. Today, except for a summary of the majority opinion, Justices often make no comment from the bench at all. They let their written opinions speak for them—and for the Court.

But there are times when a Justice feels the need to speak out. This was the case for Justice Harry Blackmun in January 1993, when the Court announced its opinion in the appeal of a convicted killer named Lionel Herrera. Herrera had asked for his death sentence to be overturned because he had new evidence that could prove him innocent. Apparently not finding the evidence persuasive, the majority of the Court decided that the prisoner, who had been on Texas's death row for some time, was too late. He had already exhausted his chances for judicial review, and could no longer present any evidence to prove his innocence. Herrera's case was rejected.

When the time came to announce the decision publicly, an outraged Justice Blackmun spoke out from the bench. By allowing the execution of a man who could show that he was innocent, Blackmun charged, the court was coming "perilously close to [committing] simple murder" itself.[10] These strong words revealed the seriousness and deep feeling that is usually hidden beneath the formal procedures and technical language of the Court.

Politics and the Court

Ideally, the highest court in the land should have nothing to do with the rough and tumble world of politics. Supreme Court Justices should act totally independently. They should not have to worry about what anyone thinks of them—not voters, not other government officials, and not anyone else. They should be concerned only with the law and not with public opinion or politics.

And, in fact, Supreme Court Justices are more protected from political concerns than any other top government officials. Everything possible is done to insulate them from any kind of political coercion. There is little anyone can do to influence the Justices. "Once we're here," a Justice once said, "they can't fire us."[1] "They" can't even cut the Justices' salaries, or take away their pensions.

The Justices are appointed for life, and so they never have to worry about being elected—or re-elected. They can leave the Court whenever they want, or serve until they die of old age. Many Justices seem reluctant to do either of those things. As a frustrated President Thomas Jefferson once complained, "few die and none resign."[2]

And yet, despite these protections, the world of politics inevitably does affect the Court. No branch of the U.S. government can ever be entirely free from the competition and compromise that are essential to democratic rule—not even the Supreme Court.

▶ Nomination to the Court

The nomination of a Supreme Court Justice is a political process. The Justices are not elected, but they are put on the Court by people who are. They first have to be nominated by the President, and then they are confirmed by the United States Senate.

The choice of a Supreme Court Justice is particularly critical because there are so few of them, and they serve for life. Presidents look for many qualities in their nominees, including personal integrity, a fine legal mind, and a solid grasp of the Constitution. But they also look for another quality that is just as important to them—political agreement.

Ever since George Washington picked John Jay to be Chief Justice, Presidents have tried to select Justices who agree with them on important legal and political questions. And why shouldn't they? Decisions of the Supreme Court help shape the history of the United States. They also help shape the success or failure of a President. A sympathetic Court can make it easier for the President to accomplish his or her plans for the country. A hostile Court, on the other hand, can block actions of the President, or strike down laws the President supports. It is only natural for Presidents to appoint Justices who share their philosophies. It would certainly be foolish for them to name Justices who would interfere with their ability to govern.

President Theodore Roosevelt put it this way: "I should hold myself as guilty of an irreparable wrong to the nation if I should put . . . [on the Court] any man who was not absolutely sane and sound on the great national policies for which we stand in public life."[3] "Sane and sound," no doubt, meant someone who agreed with President Roosevelt.

In recent years, Presidents have been attacked for setting up "litmus" tests for nominees. That is, for refusing to nominate people who disagree with them on some key issue. Because of this criticism, modern Presidents are less willing than Theodore Roosevelt to admit that they choose Justices for political or philosophical reasons. In reality, though, the choice of a Supreme Court nominee is still a political decision, and it always will be.

Presidents cannot always tell what they will get, however. The moderate Republican President Dwight Eisenhower got a big surprise when he named Earl Warren as Chief Justice in 1953. Warren had been a three-term Republican governor of California and a political supporter of the President, and Eisenhower expected him to lead a moderate if slightly progressive Court—one that would nicely match Eisenhower's administration.

But instead, Warren led the Court in a rapid and unexpected expansion of individual rights. The Warren Court quickly became the most liberal—and the most controversial—Supreme Court in modern history. Its liberal decisions outraged many conservatives, and often distressed President Eisenhower.

Some extreme conservatives publicly called Warren a traitor and demanded that he be impeached. The uproar seemed to have little effect on Warren or the other sitting Justices, who continued to make the kinds of decisions that angered conservatives. The House of Representatives also ignored the demands for impeachment, since Earl Warren had clearly not committed any impeachable crime. Nevertheless "Impeach Earl Warren" bumper stickers were common sights on cars in conservative areas of the country, from California to the Deep South.

▶ "Packing" the Court

The relationship between politics and the Supreme Court was never more clear than in 1937, when President Franklin D. Roosevelt tried to remake the Court in his own image.

The country was stuck deep in the Great Depression at the time, and the President was struggling desperately to pull it out. The national economy had collapsed. Millions of people were hungry. Homeless families wandered the roads in search of work, but there was no work for them.

Roosevelt, who was a Democrat, convinced the Congress to pass a series of liberal programs he called "The New Deal." They were designed to restart the stalled economy, and, in the meantime, to help out the millions of Americans who were suffering. The New Deal legislation included such radical measures as the AAA (Agricultural Adjustment Act), which gave the government the right to control farm production, and the NRA (National Recovery Act), which gave new rights to workers in their dealings with employers.

But most of the Supreme Court Justices of the time were elderly and conservative. Many of them had been appointed by Republican Presidents. They thought that the President was going too far in expanding governmental power. Time and again, they struck down New Deal measures, gutting the New Deal by declaring both the NRA and a key provision of the AAA unconstitutional.

Frustrated, Roosevelt announced a plan to "reform" the Court. He proposed a bill that would give him the right to expand the Court by appointing six new members. He claimed that he wanted to energize the Court by adding younger Justices. In reality, he wanted to manufacture a liberal majority that would outvote the conservatives and uphold the New Deal. Adding six new liberal

Justices to the minority of liberals already there would allow him to do just that.

The Justices already on the Court protested this interference in their authority, but there was little they could do. The Constitution gave Congress the right to set the size of the Supreme Court. Besides, this was a political battle, not a legal one. It would have to be fought in the Congress, not in the Courts.

Conservatives in the Senate accurately accused Roosevelt of trying to "pack" the Court. Liberals responded that the Court was already "packed" with aging conservatives. Even many supporters of the President were uncomfortable with his proposal, however, and in the end the Congress rejected it.

It hardly seemed to matter. Perhaps feeling that it had been warned, the Court became more open to New Deal measures. Before long, most of the older Justices had retired, and President Roosevelt eventually got to appoint the more liberal majority he had wanted all along.

▶ The Need for Advice and Consent

As the battle over the "Court-packing" plan showed, it is not the President alone who decides who should sit on the Court. According to the Constitution, the Senate must give its "advice and consent" to the President's choice. In practice, this means that the Senate votes on the nomination. If the nominee fails to win a majority of the vote in the Senate, she or he cannot sit on the high Court.

This means that it is not enough for Presidents to find nominees who agree with them. They must also pick someone the Senate will accept. When the President and the majority of the Senate belong to different political parties—as they did during most of the 1980s—such a person can be hard to find.

Senators who oppose the President are reluctant to see nominees who agree with him put on the Court. They believe that such people would make decisions that are bad for the country, and they often vote against them. At least thirty-five Supreme Court nominations have been killed in the Senate.

▶ Qualifications

The Constitution sets no qualifications for the job of Supreme Court Justices. The President could name virtually anyone he or she wanted. A Justice—even a Chief Justice—does not have to have experience as a judge, or even as a lawyer.

In practice, however, no President is likely to name a non-lawyer to the Court. If one did, the Senate would almost certainly reject the nomination. Most nominees are, in fact, highly respected members of the bar, although some have had little or no experience on the bench. Earl Warren, for example, had been a prosecutor, a Governor of California, and a Vice Presidential candidate—but not a judge—when President Eisenhower appointed him Chief Justice.

▶ The Confirmation Process

At one time, the Senate voted on Supreme Court nominations with a simple voice vote. Today, however, the confirmation process is more complicated.

There is usually an investigation of the nominee by the staff of the Senate Judiciary Committee. The committee also gets a report from the American Bar Association, the main association of attorneys in the country, evaluating the nominee's legal background.

Committee hearings are then held, at which witnesses—including the nominee—are questioned by senators from both political parties. When they are finished, the committee votes on whether or not to recommend that the full Senate accept the nomination. It is only after receiving the committee's recommendation that the full Senate votes on the nomination.

▶ "Borking" a Nominee

Committee hearings can be rough. These days, they are televised, and senators who oppose nominees use the cameras to present a case against them to the viewers. A lot is at stake, and the attacks on nominees can become both intense and personal.

In modern times, most nominees have tried to be as low key and noncontroversial as possible in their testimony. In 1987, however, Judge Robert Bork chose to be combative. A leading spokesperson for the conservative political and legal philosophy, Bork, who was a federal judge, was nominated by the conservative Republican President Ronald Reagan. When liberal—and politically hostile—Democrats on the Senate Judiciary Committee questioned him about his opinions, Bork decided to debate with them.

Although Bork was widely respected in legal

circles, the senators seized the chance to hold his views up to public ridicule. They treated those ideas—and to some extent, Bork himself—as radical and eccentric. In the end, his nomination was rejected by the Senate.

His defeat added a new word to the political dictionary, as conservatives complained that the nominee had been "borked." Since then, nominees fearful of being "borked" themselves have stubbornly refused to discuss their political and legal opinions in detail with the committee. This makes it harder for opponents to make their philosophies a major issue in the nomination process.

▶ Questions of Character

In theory, senators can oppose a nominee for any reason at all, including the nominee's political ideology. There is, however, a general feeling that Presidents are entitled to appoint Justices who agree with them, provided that their opinions are not too far out of the mainstream. For this reasons, some senators are reluctant to admit that they oppose a nominee because they disagree with the President's choice politically. They look for other reasons to turn down the nominee: questioning his or her legal qualifications, integrity, or even personal morality.

The Bork defeat left a bad taste in the mouth of many Americans who felt that Supreme Court nominations should somehow be above politics. The liberal senators on the Judiciary Committee were criticized by some for going too far—for being too political.

So, when President Reagan named a new nominee, Judge Douglas Ginsburg, the liberals on the committee were reluctant to reject him for his political views. And yet, they were equally reluctant to put a Reagan conservative on the Court.

So instead of attacking him solely for his beliefs, they took a different tack. They raised questions about his financial dealings, and they argued Ginsburg had a lack of legal experience. Ginsburg was surviving these attacks until revelations that he had smoked marijuana while a law professor at Harvard University finally scuttled his nomination.

By the time Reagan's third nominee, a federal judge named Anthony Kennedy, reached the Senate, there was a feeling that the liberals had done as much as they could politically. Defeating another conservative nominee might have resulted in a backlash against the senators themselves. Kennedy sailed through the nomination process with little real opposition.

In 1991, however, another conservative nominee, Judge Clarence Thomas, found his sexual morality under attack by liberal members of the committee. A young female law professor named Anita Hill charged him with sexually harassing her when she had worked for him some years before. Thomas angrily denied her claim.

The televised confirmation hearings became a kind of soap opera. Tens of millions of Americans watched in fascination, as senators questioned Hill and Thomas about personal sexual matters. Each accused the other of lying. Although there was no way to know for sure who was telling the truth, many viewers took sides. Professor Hill became a heroine to feminists, while Judge Thomas became a hero to conservatives.

Thomas, who, like Hill, is an African American, bitterly denounced the hearings as a public "lynching." Some legal experts questioned whether the charges against him had anything to do with his fitness to serve on the Court. After all, even if Hill's claims were true, he had broken no law, and the accusations had nothing to do with his ability to make legal decisions. In the end, he was confirmed by a vote of 52 to 48 in the Senate.

▶ The Threat of Impeachment

No matter how frustrated Presidents, members of Congress, or the public may be, the Constitution protects Justices from being removed unless they commit some "high crime or misdemeanor," such as treason or bribery. Even then, they have to be impeached (charged) by the U.S. House of Representatives and convicted in a trial held by the Senate.

No Justice has ever been thrown off the Court in this way. Only one, Samuel Chase, was ever even tried by the Senate, and that took place way back in 1805. Chase was a distinguished judge, but he was also a fiercely political Federalist, and an enemy of the Democratic policies and ideals of President Thomas Jefferson.

As a sitting judge as well as a Supreme Court

Justice, Chase had a reputation for coming down hard on unlucky Jeffersonians who found themselves in his Court. When he used a charge to a Baltimore grand jury to accuse the Democrats of leading the country toward "mobocracy," President Jefferson had had enough of the quarrelsome judge. He encouraged Democrats in the House to impeach Chase and send him to the Senate for trial.[4] In essence, Chase was being charged with opposing the policies of the President and the Democratic Congress. Only the staunchest Democrats believed that this was the kind of crime the Constitution had in mind when it set up the standards for impeachment.

Chase's trial became a test of the independence of the judiciary—a test that was almost failed. Although even some Jeffersonians voted to acquit him, the majority of senators voted to throw Chase off the Court. Fortunately for him—and for the future independence of the Court—the total fell short of the two-thirds needed to convict. Chase stayed on the Court, and the Jeffersonians abandoned the idea of impeaching Federalist judges.

Even so, the case of Samuel Chase served as a caution to Justices to watch their tongue when talking politics. Most of them have been careful to follow that caution ever since.

Although no Justice since Chase has been impeached by the House, several Justices have come under heavy political pressure. For at least one, Abe Fortas, the pressure was heavy enough to force him to resign.

▶ The Resignation of Justice Fortas

Justice Fortas was one of the most prominent members of the Warren Court. A friend and political ally of the Democratic President who appointed him, Lyndon Johnson, he was Johnson's choice to become Chief Justice when Earl Warren retired in 1968. That required him to undergo new Senate confirmation hearings, however, and they did not go well.

Conservative senators, angry at the rulings of the Warren Court, took the opportunity to revenge themselves on one of the Court's most liberal

Justice Abe Fortas was one of the most prominent members of the Warren Court, but he came under attack in 1968 during new Senate confirmation hearings.

members. Among other things, they attacked Fortas for accepting a large sum of money from a charity run by an old client. This was not actually illegal, but it seemed to throw some doubt on Fortas's financial ethics. He withdrew his nomination for Chief Justice.

The next year, Fortas came under fire again. *Life* magazine reported new charges of shady financial dealings with another ex-client. The new Republican President, Richard Nixon, was eager to appoint conservatives to the Court, and Republicans did what they could to add fuel to the flames. With Johnson out of office, no one was left to defend Fortas. With his reputation—and the honor of the Supreme Court—under attack, Fortas resigned.

The Fortas case made clear that even Supreme Court Justices are not entirely safe from political pressure or from personal disgrace. But Fortas's resignation was more than a personal humiliation. It led to a major shift in the direction of the Supreme Court. The man President Nixon chose to replace Fortas was Warren Burger, who would become Chief Justice and preside over the transformation of the liberal Court headed by Earl Warren to the much more conservative Court we still have today.

Historic
Decisions

The work of the Supreme Court often seems dry, dull, and distant from the lives of most Americans. Much of it consists of disputes over legal language, or applying the technical details of complicated laws to obscure cases. Only very rarely is it intensely dramatic, as when the Court hears a last minute appeal from a prisoner on death row.

And yet, what the Supreme Court does affects us all. Decisions of the Supreme Court have transformed virtually every aspect of American society. The following are just some of the many historic decisions of the Supreme Court.

▶ *Scott v. Sandford*[1]—Inspiring Civil War

The Dred Scott case, as it is usually known, began in 1846 when abolitionists encouraged a slave of that name to ask a state court in Missouri to free him and his wife. Although Missouri was a slave state, Missouri courts had ruled that only people born into slavery would be considered slaves in Missouri. Once a person was free, they could never be enslaved.

The Scotts' master had taken them with him when he visited the state of Illinois and the Wisconsin Territory. Since slavery was illegal in both places, the Scotts' lawyer argued, the Scotts were legally free during those visits. Therefore, they must still be free under Missouri law. A Missouri court agreed in 1850, but the Missouri Supreme Court overruled that decision in 1852, and declared that Dred Scott was still a slave.

The case was appealed to the Supreme Court. Speaking for the majority of the Court, Chief Justice Roger Taney ruled that the Missouri Supreme Court had been right. Scott was still a slave. Slaves were property, and slaveowners had the right to take their property with them from state to state.

Taney went even further. The suit, he declared, should never have been brought in the first place. Blacks were not citizens of the United States, and so Scott had no right to sue. In fact, he had no rights at all. Slave or free, Taney insisted, a black person had "no rights which the white man was bound to respect."

Although the *Scott* decision delighted southern slaveowners, its political impact was the opposite of what they expected it to be. Instead of confirming the rights of slaveowners in the minds of all

Americans, it inflamed antislavery feeling in the North. It convinced even moderate northerners that there could be no compromise with the slave states, and so helped bring on both the Civil War and the end of slavery itself.

The *Scott* decision reminds us that Supreme Court is not always right. It can sometimes be horribly and tragically wrong. As the ex-slave Frederick Douglass wrote in the wake of the hateful decision:

> The Supreme Court is not the only power in this world. It is very great, but the Supreme Court of the Almighty is greater. [The Court] can do many things, but [it] cannot perform impossibilities... [It] cannot change the essential nature of things— making evil good, and good, evil.[2]

▶ *Ex Parte Milligan*[3]—Putting a Limit on Government Power

It is generally accepted that the government needs emergency powers in wartime. Such powers frequently infringe upon the civil rights that we take for granted in times of peace. Somehow, those rights seem less important when the safety of U.S. troops—and the future of the country itself—is at stake.

In wartime, the U.S. government has done many things that it would never do in times of peace. It has taken over private businesses and converted them to making weapons, and it has closed down newspapers hostile to the war effort. During World War II, it even imprisoned thousands of innocent American citizens of Japanese descent for fear that they might help Japan during the war. And the courts have generally approved these measures, allowing the government to do whatever it thought it needed to do to win the war.

But does that mean that there is *no* judicial check on the enormous war powers of the federal government? Does a threat to the nation's security justify *any* abuse of civil rights, whether necessary or not? According to the Supreme Court, the answer is no.

This principle grew out of a case from the United States' most desperate war—the War Between the States. Late in that conflict, U.S. Army forces arrested three anti-Union Democrats in Indiana. The Army suspected the men, who were Confederate sympathizers, of plotting to steal government weapons and release prisoners held in Union prison camps. Afraid that civilian juries in that heavily Democratic area would be sympathetic to the defendants, the Army tried the men in its own courts, according to military law. They were convicted and sentenced to death.

One of the condemned men, Lambdin Milligan, appealed to the U.S. Circuit Court in Indiana. He argued that he was a civilian, subject to civilian law. The military had had no right to try him under military law. When the case eventually reached the U.S. Supreme Court, that Court ordered Milligan and his companions released. The nine Justices gave different reasons for their decision, but they were unanimous in the result. Civilian courts had been operating in Indiana at the time, and that is where the conspirators should have been tried.

As in so many great decisions of the Supreme Court, the actual outcome of the case was not important but the principle the decision established was. Even in wartime, the Court was saying, the powers of the government are not absolute. As much as possible, the rights of the citizens must be protected—even those citizens suspected of treason. The Constitution, as Justice David Davis wrote in his decision, is "a law for rulers and people, equally in times of war and peace."

▶ *Plessy* v. *Ferguson*[4]—Allowing Segregation

The Thirteenth Amendment had freed the slaves, and the Fourteenth Amendment promised "equal protection of the law" to all Americans, whatever their color. Nonetheless, those rights were consistently denied to most African Americans in the late nineteenth century, particularly in the South.

The system of legalized segregation, called Jim Crow, required "coloreds" to use different public accommodations than "whites"—to attend different schools, eat in different restaurants, use different public toilets, and so on.

In 1896, a "white"-skinned man named Plessy challenged a state law that made it necessary for "coloreds" to ride in "equal but separate" passenger cars on the railroads in Louisiana. Despite his light skin, Plessy was legally "colored" under the Jim Crow laws because he had an African-American grandparent.

Plessy was not, in fact, acting alone. He represented a committee of New Orleans citizens of mixed and African-American parentage who hoped to have the segregation law ruled unconstitutional under both the Thirteenth and Fourteenth Amendments. But, by a vote of 8 to 1, the Supreme Court refused to do so.

Segregation was constitutional, declared Justice Henry Billings Brown in his decision. It did not violate the Thirteenth Amendment because it did nothing to bring back slavery. And it did not violate the Fourteenth Amendment, either, as long as the facilities used by blacks were "equal" to those used by whites, segregation did not imply that either race was inferior. The only dissenter to this unfortunate ruling was Justice John Marshall Harlan, who insisted that the "Constitution is color-blind."

The Court's ruling in *Plessy* firmly established the legality of "separate but equal" facilities for African Americans in the South. Because of it, segregation would continue to exist throughout the region until the Court finally rejected the doctrine of "separate but equal" in the *Brown* v. *Board of Education* case nearly sixty years later. In the meantime, three generations of African Americans would be forced to live under the indignities of Jim Crow.

▶ *Heart of Atlanta Motel* v. *United States*[5]—Enforcing Civil Rights

The Supreme Court's power is most obvious when it is used to strike down a law or to cancel actions taken by other branches of the government. But the Court is just as important when it affirms what other branches do. Even after a controversial law is passed by Congress and signed by the President, a haunting question sometimes remains. Is this really Constitutional?

Demanding that controversial laws be overturned, citizens who disagree with them often attack them on Constitutional grounds. In a sense, then, no law that raises Constitutional issues can be considered completely legitimate until the Supreme Court accepts it.

A striking example of this occurred in the mid-1960s, when President Lyndon Johnson pressured Congress into passing a sweeping law that finally guaranteed the civil rights of African Americans. Known as the Civil Rights Act of 1964, it was a direct attack on what remained of Jim Crow. It formally outlawed racial discrimination not only in public accommodations but in employment and other areas of life as well.

Passage of the law did not immediately end segregation, however. Many white businesses continued to refuse to hire African Americans, as well as refusing to serve them in "whites only" restaurants, hotels, and other business establishments. Congress, they argued, had no right to tell them whom they could serve in their own businesses.

One of these white businesspeople was the owner of the Heart of Atlanta Motel. He insisted that the Civil Rights Act requiring him to serve African Americans overstepped Congress's power to regulate business, and that it was a violation of the Fifth and Thirteenth Amendments. When a U.S. District

Court ordered him to stop turning away travelers because they were black, he appealed to the Supreme Court. In a 9 to 0 decision, the Court affirmed the U.S. District Court and established the constitutionality of the Civil Rights Act of 1964.

Congress, the Court said, had the right under its police powers to pass laws against such moral wrongs as racial discrimination—and no citizen had the right to disobey them.

Many whites would continue to resist the end of segregation, but they could no longer claim that they had any legal right to do so.

▶ *Near* v. *Minnesota*[6]—Protecting Freedom Of the Press

One of the things that sets the United States apart from most other countries is the rare freedom its press enjoys. Many countries have much stricter laws regulating what people can say in print or on the air. In some countries, the government controls the press almost completely. Nothing controversial can be published without government approval *in advance.* This means that the government can keep the people from finding out anything the government does not want them to know.

Even here, freedom of the press is not absolute. For example, obscenity (material which appeals solely to an unhealthy or morbid interest in sex) and libel (the deliberate damaging of another person's reputation by publishing lies) are both forbidden. Anyone found guilty of publishing obscene or libelous material can be punished, but only after being found guilty in a court of law. Obscenity can, in effect, be a criminal offense, punishable by imprisonment and/or a fine. Libel, on the other hand, is a civil matter, and the offending party can be sued.

However, the Supreme Court insists that the First Amendment guarantees that there can be no punishment at all for the expression of political opinions. But there was a time when this protection was in danger. Like so many other countries, the United States might have fallen victim to government control of the press.

In 1925, the state of Minnesota passed a law that gave the judges the right to prevent publication of anything they considered "lewd" or "scandalous." But when a judge tried to stop a weekly Minneapolis newspaper run by J.M. Near from publishing a story exposing corruption in the city, Near appealed to the U.S. Supreme Court.

By a vote of 5 to 4, the Court ruled that this "prior restraint" of the press—in which the government forbids the publication of something in advance—was unconstitutional. The Court admitted that there might be some truly exceptional situation in which prior restraint was justified. However, ordinarily, it insisted, the state has no right to interfere with the press's freedom to publish.

This ruling did not so much protect a certain kind of speech as it limited the way in which potentially objectionable material could be censored. Libel and obscenity can still be punished with civil or criminal sanctions, but only after they have been published. Society must have had a chance to judge it, and the due process of the law must have been followed. The government does not have the power to review things in advance, and therefore to decide what the American public will be allowed to see and hear.

▶ *Mapp v. Ohio*[7]—Making Local Authorities Obey the Constitution

One of the ongoing challenges for the U.S. Supreme Court is to decide how state and federal laws affect each other, and particularly how the U.S. Constitution applies to the states. That was the underlying issue in this case involving the arrest of a Cleveland woman for possession of obscene materials.

It began with a sordid little local incident in 1957, when Cleveland police barged into a boarding-house run by Dolly Mapp. The police had heard there was illegal gambling equipment in Mapp's place and that a criminal fugitive was hiding out there. As it turned out, they found neither one, but they did come across some printed material they decided was pornographic. They charged Mapp with possession of obscene materials. She was convicted, but she appealed, and the case eventually reached the Supreme Court in 1961.

It hardly seemed like the sort of case on which a great constitutional issue would ride. But there was, in fact, a great issue at stake. Did the Fourth Amendment, which protects citizens against "unreasonable searches and seizures" by the federal government, fully apply to local officials as well?

Ordinarily, police need a warrant to enter a person's home uninvited. That warrant, authorized by a judge, gives them the power to search for specific evidence. The police who broke into Dolly Mapp's house told her that they had such a warrant, but they would not show it to her. Even if they did have one, however, it would have been to look for gambling equipment and fugitives, not for pornography. Mapp's attorney argued that this made the search "unreasonable."

If the search had been conducted by federal law enforcement officials, the Court would definitely have thrown out the conviction on Fourth Amendment grounds. In the case of *Weeks* v. *United States* in 1914, the Court had already ruled that federal officials could not use evidence gathered in an "unreasonable search or seizure to convict anyone of anything. But did this so called "exclusionary rule" apply to searches conducted by local officials as well? Did state courts have to abide by it?

By a vote of 5 to 4, the Court decided that they did. It threw out Dolly Mapp's conviction and established that the "exclusionary rule" protects defendants in state as well as federal courts.

Mapp changed the way police have to behave all over the country. It was—and still is—an extremely controversial decision. Some law enforcement officials insist that it ties their hands and sets guilty criminals free. Even Justice Tom Clark, who wrote the majority opinion in *Mapp*, agreed that this might happen. But, he insisted, the rule of law, as governed by the Constitution, is more important than the fate of a particular criminal. "The criminal goes free if he must," Clark wrote, "but it is the law that sets him free."

▶ *Miranda* v. *Arizona*[8]—Protecting Suspects Against Self-incrimination

Every watcher of TV cop shows has seen it happen over and over again. A police officer arrests someone, and reads the suspect his or her "rights." "You have the right to remain silent . . ." This is not something made up by television scriptwriters. Real-life police do the same thing. They have to—thanks to a decision of the Supreme Court.

The Constitution tries to protect people from being forced to incriminate themselves in a crime. The Fifth Amendment guarantees that no one shall be "compelled . . . to be a witness against himself," and the Sixth Amendment guarantees an accused person "the Assistance of Counsel for his defense." But what do these rights actually mean to an ordinary citizen arrested for a crime?

Being arrested is a shocking experience for most people. Snatched from their ordinary lives and hauled to a police station for questioning, criminal suspects often become frightened and confused. Isolated in a room with several police officers who can be very intimidating, they may be questioned for hour after hour. Under such circumstances, they are apt to say things that will haunt them later. Many make mistakes in the information they give. They may deliberately lie to the police in obvious ways that cast doubt on everything they say. Or they may feel so threatened that they break down and confess—sometimes admitting to things they did not even do.

This might have happened to a down and out Phoenix resident named Ernesto Miranda. A twenty-three-year-old who had never made it to senior high school, Miranda had been arrested for kidnapping and raping a teenaged girl. After being questioned for two hours in a Phoenix police station, Miranda had written out a confession in his own hand. He had then been convicted, partly on the basis of that confession.

Miranda appealed, arguing that he had been "compelled" to answer the police's questions by the circumstances under which he had been arrested and held. By a vote of 5 to 4, the Court threw out Miranda's conviction. No one had told him that he did not have to answer the police's questions, nor had anyone said that he had a right to a lawyer even though he could not pay for one. Any good lawyer would have told him not to talk to the police. In effect, he had been unconstitutionally pressured into incriminating himself with his handwritten confession. Whether the confession was true or false was not relevant to the principle involved. The rights enshrined in the Constitution are vital. If the police can get confessions by keeping suspects ignorant of their constitutional rights, those rights become meaningless.

In the past, the Fifth Amendment had only been enforced in the courtroom, where defendants were excused from testifying in their own cases if they did not choose to. In the future, the Court now ruled, it would apply in police stations and other official interrogations as well.

Before being questioned, suspected criminals would now have to be informed of four facts: 1) they have the right to remain silent; 2) if they choose to speak, anything they say can and will be used against them; 3) they have a right to see a lawyer before questioning, and to have the lawyer with them whenever they are questioned; and 4) if they cannot afford a lawyer, one will be provided for them.

The *Miranda* decision angered many police officers and prosecutors alike. They feared that suspects who were informed of their rights would refuse to speak. Confessions would be harder to get, and the number of criminal convictions would fall. Despite their fears, however, many criminals still confess, and convictions rates do not seem to have suffered.

Ever since the *Miranda* decision, police officers have carried the four so-called Miranda warnings written on small cards in their pockets. In order to make sure that the correct warnings are given, they read them off to suspects when placing them under arrest.

Ernesto Miranda used to carry the cards, too. They made him a minor celebrity in the sleazy Phoenix neighborhood where he hung out. When he was killed in a bar fight in 1976, ten years after the historic decision, the police found two of the cards in his pocket. They used one of them to read the Miranda warnings to the man suspected of killing him.[9]

▶ Reed v. Reed[10]—Making Sex Discrimination a Constitutional Question

For much of the past century, women of *all* colors were more discriminated against in many ways than men of *any* color. For a long time, unmarried women were legally considered almost the property of their fathers, and married women were at the mercy of their husbands. Until 1920, most women could not even vote. Even after that, high paying jobs were routinely denied to women. It was simply assumed that they were not strong enough, intelligent enough, or stable enough to perform them.

For many decades, the Supreme Court went along with this discrimination against women, just as it did with discrimination against African Americans. In 1876, for instance, it allowed Illinois to keep women from practicing law. In 1948, it upheld a law forbidding women to serve as bartenders (unless they were working in bars owned by their husbands or fathers). Like most other males in the United States, the Supreme Court Justices believed that there were sound, rational reasons for the laws that discriminated between men and women.

It was not until 1971 that the Court finally decided that there was an important constitutional issue at stake when women were discriminated against under the law. The case involved an Idaho law that laid down who should administer the estates of people who died without a will. It listed several categories of relatives in order. When both a male and a female relative were available, the man was to be chosen over the woman.

For the first time in history—by the surprisingly unanimous vote of 9 to 0—the Court ruled in favor of the woman in a sexual discrimination case. The Idaho law, said the Court, violated the Fourteenth Amendment, which guarantees all people "the equal protection of the laws."

The *Reed* decision did not forbid all sex discrimination. The Court still assumes that there are acceptable reasons for making some legal differences between men and women. So far, for example, it has refused to interfere with the U.S. military's refusal to put women into front-line combat positions.

Even so, *Reed* was a major breakthrough for the cause of women's rights. It opened the way for constitutional challenges to a wide range of discriminatory laws and regulations, and many of those challenges have succeeded.

▶ *Roe v. Wade*[11]—Allowing Abortion

The early 1970s was a critical time for "women's issues" before the Court. Two years after deciding that sexual discrimination was a constitutional question in *Reed*, the Court finally agreed to decide if abortion was a constitutional question as well.

At that time, most of the states had laws banning abortion that had stood for at least a century. Many churches condemned the practice as immoral, and millions of Americans thought of it as a form of murder. Anti-abortion activists, who proclaimed themselves "pro life," argued that a baby was a human being from the moment of conception. The state, they said, had a duty to protect the life of the unborn.

But a growing number of "pro choice" women and men were insisting that it was wrong for society to force women to give birth to babies they did not want. Besides, they insisted, the unborn was only a fetus, and not yet a baby. Full human life did not begin until the child was able to live on its own outside the mother's womb. So long as the fetus was inside a woman's body, it should be her decision, and no one else's, whether or not to give birth to it.

These arguments, and the extremely effective "pro choice" political movement that made them, convinced several states to liberalize their laws and grant women the right to have abortions under certain circumstances. If the pregnancy was the result of rape, for example, or if giving birth would present a serious risk to the life of the mother, abortions were now allowed in some states. But some states continued to ban virtually all abortions, no matter what the circumstances. One of those was Texas.

Using the name Jane Roe to hide her identity, a pregnant Texan woman appealed to the courts for the right to abort. The Supreme Court eventually agreed to hear her case, as well as another one asking the Court to overturn another state's anti-abortion law. By a vote of 7 to 2, the Court overturned both laws.

Writing for the majority, Justice Harry Blackmun

declared that the laws violated women's right to privacy. In other words, the decision of whether or not to have an abortion was, at least to some extent, a private one. No right to privacy is mentioned directly in the Constitution, but Blackmun ruled that it was implied by the Fourteenth Amendment's guarantee of "due process" under the law.

Although the *Roe* decision established a privacy right to abortion, it also established that that right was not absolute. At some point in the process a baby was clearly present, and at that point at least, the state would have an interest in protecting its life. Just how strong that interest was, and when it began, were not entirely clear.

The longer the pregnancy went on, however, the more interest the state might have in protecting the unborn. During the first trimester (three months) of pregnancy, the state had almost no right to limit the right to abortion. During the second trimester, it could begin to restrict that right to protect the unborn. During the final three months of pregnancy, the state could set many restrictions to protect the life of the unborn, unless preventing an abortion would result in the death of the mother.

Roe was one of the most controversial Court decisions of this century. Some "right to choose" groups object to putting any limits on a woman's right to abort, while the "right to life" forces object to allowing abortions under any circumstances at all. Many doctors contest the scientific basis for treating pregnancy differently in different trimesters.

In the wake of the *Roe* decision, however, many states rushed to pass laws that limit abortion only in ways that might satisfy the Court. Some of these restrictions have been upheld and some have been rejected. For a time, it seemed that the Court's recent conservative majority might overturn *Roe* altogether. But that has not happened. The practical significance of *Roe* is unquestioned. For better or worse, legal abortions now number more than one-and-one-half million each year.

Decisions like the ones discussed in this book do much more than answer abstract legal questions, or determine the outcome of particular cases.

They touch the lives of all Americans—sometimes for good, and sometimes for bad.

They alter the relationship between the people of the United States and their government.

They change the course of history.

And, most important of all, they help to shape our nation, and to define its ideals.

They make us what we are.

Glossary

appeal—A request to a higher court, from the losing party in a criminal or civil case, for it to review and reverse the decision of a lower court.

appellate court—A so-called higher court, which hears appeals from decisions made by lower courts.

Associate Justice—One of the eight ordinary Justices of the United States Supreme Court, each of whose vote on a case is equal to that of the Chief Justice.

Chief Justice—The office of Chief Justice was established by the United States Constitution, although most of its responsibilities have been established by tradition. In addition to presiding over Court proceedings, the Chief Justice has a variety of administrative, managerial, and public relations duties.

civil cases—Cases in which one private party sues another for damages. The punishment in civil cases is usually monetary.

concurring opinion—An opinion issued by a Justice of the U.S. Supreme Court that agrees with the ultimate decision reached by the majority opinion, but gives somewhat different reasons for reaching that decision.

Court of Appeals (U.S.)—Circuit courts that hear appeals from decisions of the lower federal courts. There are thirteen federal circuits around the country, in addition to a Temporary Emergency Court of Appeals. Since they are not trial courts, they have no juries.

criminal cases—Cases involving alleged violations of the criminal law. The accusing party in a criminal case is either a state or the federal government. Punishment is usually a fine, imprisonment, or both.

defendant—The party accused in a criminal trial or sued in a civil lawsuit.

dissenting opinion—An opinion issued by a Justice of the U.S. Supreme Court stating the Justice's reasons for disagreeing with the majority opinion in a case.

district court—One of the trial courts of the federal system. There is at least one district court in each state.

due process of law—A constitutional right, established by the Fifth Amendment, that assures all individuals will be treated fairly according to the laws of the United States.

judge—A public official with the authority to hear and decide criminal and/or civil cases. In jury trials, it is the job of the judge to rule on the law, while the jury decides the facts. In cases heard without juries, the judge fulfills both functions. Higher court judges hear and decide appeals from lower courts.

jury—A group of ordinary citizens picked to listen to the evidence in a criminal or civil trial and determine what the facts are.

opinion—A written decision in a case before the U.S. Supreme Court. The opinion of the Court is written by a Justice assigned to do so by the Chief Justice, if he or she is in the majority, or by the senior Justice on the majority side. In addition, each Justice is free to write his or her own opinion, either concurring with or dissenting from the decision of the Court.

plaintiff—The accusing party in a lawsuit.

precedent—A previous ruling establishing a legal interpretation or practice. Judges often rely on such past decisions to guide them in current cases.

seriatim opinions—Separate, individual opinions written by each Justice in ruling on a case. Seriatim opinions were customary until Chief Justice Marshall convinced the Justices to abandon them in favor of a single opinion expressing the decision of the Court. Justices still often write their own concurring or dissenting opinions, however.

State Supreme Court—The highest court in a particular state, which has the power to overrule the lower state courts in certain instances; in Maryland and New York, it is called the Court of Appeals.

trial—A legal proceeding, conducted in front of a judge and/or a jury, to determine the facts of a matter under dispute. The matter can be either criminal or civil, depending on the nature of the allegations. At the end of the trial, either a criminal punishment or civil penalty may be assessed.

writ of certiorari—("To make more certain.") An order from the Supreme Court for a lower court to send up the record of a case for review.

Chapter Notes

Supreme Court decisions are listed by their names, followed by a citation of where to find them in the official volumes known as *United States Reports*, in which the decisions of the Court are published. The first number refers to the number of the volume containing the particular case; "U.S." is simply short for *United States Reports;* the second number gives the page at which the report of the decision begins; and the number in parentheses refers to the year in which the case was decided.

Preface
1. Mary Ann Harrell and Burnett Anderson, *Equal Justice Under Law: The Supreme Court in American Life* (Washington, D.C.: The Supreme Court Historical Society, 1988), p. 123.

Chapter 1
1. *Brown* v. *Board of Education*, 347 U.S. 483 (1954).

Chapter 2
1. Mary Ann Harrell and Burnett Anderson, *Equal Justice Under Law: The Supreme Court in American Life* (Washington, D.C.: The Supreme Court Historical Society, 1988), p. 142.

Chapter 3
1. Alan Green, *Justice For All* (Washington, D.C.: C-Span, 1987), pp. 11–12.

2. Ibid., p. 12.

3. Kermit L. Hall, *The Oxford Companion to the Supreme Court of the United States* (New York: Oxford University Press, 1992), p. 447.

4. *Marbury* v. *Madison*, 5 U.S. 137 (1803).

5. Green, p. 12.

6. *Charles River Bridge* v. *Warren Bridge*, 36 U.S. 420 (1837).

7. Hall, p. 855.

8. Brandeis dissent, *Olmstead* v. *U.S.*, 277 U.S. 438 (1928).

9. *Roe* v. *Wade*, 410 U.S. 113 (1973).

10. *Furman* v. *Georgia*, 408 U.S. 238 (1972).

11. *Gregg* v. *Georgia*, 428 U.S. 153 (1976).

12. Jeffrey Rosen, "The List," *The New Republic*, May 10, 1993, p. 15.

Chapter 4

1. Mark S. Hoffman, ed., *World Almanac and Book of Facts 1993*, (New York: World Almanac, 1992), p. 158.

2. Terry Eastman, quoted by Herbert Buchsbaum in "The Kids on the Court," *Scholastic Update*, September 17, 1993, p. 10.

3. Kermit L. Hall, ed., *The Oxford Companion to the Supreme Court of the United States*, (New York: Oxford University Press, 1992), p. 428.

4. *Gideon* v. *Wainwright*, 372 U.S. 335 (1963).

5. Hall, p. 132.

6. Larry Elowitz, *Introduction to Government* (New York: Harper, 1992), p. 137.

7. *Nightline*, ABC-TV, Dec. 2, 1993.

8. Peter Irons and Stephanie Guitton, eds., *May It Please the Court*, (New York: The New Press, 1993), p. 84.

9. Ibid., p. 173.

10. Dennis Cauchon, "Court: Late Evidence May Not Halt Execution," *USA Today*, January 26, 1993.

Chapter 5

1. Mary Ann Harrell and Burnett Anderson, *Equal Justice Under Law: The Supreme Court in American Life* (Washington, D.C.: The Supreme Court Historical Society, 1988), p. 126.

2. Kermit L. Hall, ed., *The Oxford Companion to the Supreme Court of the United States*, (New York: Oxford University Press, 1992), p. 855.

3. Hiller B. Zobel, "Naming a Justice: It Has Always Been Politics as Usual," *American Heritage*, October 1991, p. 98.

4. Richard N. Current, T. Harry Williams, and Frank Freidel, *American History: A Survey*, fourth edition (New York: Alfred A. Knopf, 1975), p. 192.

Chapter 6

1. *Dred Scott* v. *John F. A. Sandford*, 60 U.S. 393 (1857).

2. "Frederick Douglass on the Dred Scott Decision, May 14, 1857," from *Two Speeches by Frederick Douglass* (Rochester, N.Y., 1857), excerpted in *Voices of the American Past*, Morton Borden, ed. (Lexington, Mass.: D.C. Health, 1972), pp. 166–167.

3. *Ex parte Milligan*, 71 U.S. 2 (1866).

4. *Plessy* v. *Ferguson*, 163 U.S. 537 (1896).

5. *Heart of Atlanta Motel* v. *United States*, 379 U.S. 241 (1964).

6. *Near* v. *Minnesota*, 283 U.S. 697 (1931).

7. *Mapp* v. *Ohio*, 367 U.S. 643 (1961).

8. *Miranda* v. *Arizona*, 384 U.S. 436 (1966).

9. Jethro K. Lieberman, *The Evolving Constitution* (New York: Random House, 1992), p. 332.

10. *Reed* v. *Reed*, 404 U.S. 71 (1971).

11. *Roe* v. *Wade*, 410 U.S. 113 (1973).

Further Reading

Fisher, Louis. *Constitutional Conflicts Between Congress and the President*. 3rd edition. Lawrence, Kansas: University Press of Kansas, 1991.

Hall, Kermit L., ed., *The Oxford Companion to the Supreme Court of the United States*. New York: Oxford University Press, 1992.

Harrell, Mary Ann, and Burnett Anderson. *Equal Justice Under Law: The Supreme Court in American Life*. Washington, D.C.: The Supreme Court Historical Society, 1988.

Lewis, Anthony, *Make No Law.* New York: Random House, 1991.

Lieberman, Jethro K. *The Evolving Constitution.* New York: Random House, 1992.

O'Brien, David M., *Storm Center: The Supreme Court in American Politics*. New York: Norton, 1986.

Pfeffer, Leo. *This Honorable Court: A History of the United States Supreme Court*. Boston: Beacon Press, 1965.

Rehnquist, William. *The Supreme Court: How It Was, How It Is.* New York: William Morrow & Co., 1987.

Tribe, Laurence H. *God Save This Honorable Court.* New York: Random House, 1985.

Index